...and they walked away!

This edition first published in 2004 by Motorbooks International, an imprint of MBI Publishing Company, Galtier Plaza, Suite 200, 380 Jackson Street, St. Paul, MN 55101-3885 USA

Motorbooks International titles are also available at discounts in bulk quantity for industrial or sales-promotional use. For details write to Special Sales Manager at Motorbooks International Wholesalers & Distributors, Galtier Plaza, Suite 200, 380 Jackson Street, St. Paul, MN 55101-3885 USA.

ISBN 0-7603-1944-8

Printed in China

All photographs come from the LAT Photographic Archive, the world's leading photographic library with more than 9.5 million photographic images in stock covering every form of motorsport from Formula 1 to rallying to NASCAR, but also including Indycars, touring cars, club racing and historics, dating all the way back to when racing began, in 1895. Peter Higham headed the project of sourcing the images used in this book, with assistance from Tim Wright and Jeff Bloxham. LAT is based in Teddington, Middlesex, England.

...and they walked away!

Bruce Jones

MOTORBOOKS
INTERNATIONAL

CONTENTS

"If he'd given me space, there'd have been no problem. I'm sorry about the consequences"

Gabriele Tarquini

INTRODUCTION

Motorsport can be dangerous. All fans of racing and rallying know that. Indeed, it's part of the attraction, as without the spills there wouldn't be so many thrills. Motorsport in all of its forms is spectacular and we all love the screech of tyres, the sight of tyres smoking and a car sliding sideways or even spinning, especially if this happens in the heat of battle. If we're being honest, a driver losing control gets the adrenalin flowing like nothing else, but only as long as the drivers concerned come out of it shaken but not stirred. This frisson of danger and the anticipation as to when a dicing duo will change order or clash in so doing makes the competition that we love all the more gladiatorial.

Thankfully, modern technology and an ongoing campaign for greater safety has led to a massive reduction in injury and even death, enabling drivers to pop their belts after a big impact, clamber out of their wrecked machinery, salute the fans and walk away. Their forerunners were not so fortunate, with scarcely a weekend passing in the 1950s and 1960s without another driver "buying the farm." It's not just the cars that are safer now, but the circuits too, with gravel traps, debris fencing, walls and crash barriers keeping the cars and drivers away from the scenery. No more do race tracks thread their way through forests with nothing other than thin air separating the drivers from the trees.

The statistics of driver fatalities made incredibly grim reading several decades ago, so we must all raise our hats to those who have campaigned so hard to develop roll cages that can keep touring car or NASCAR drivers alike secure in their cocoon in a major collision. It has always been a tougher job protecting single-seater drivers in the case of a major impact, such is the exposure of their head and shoulders, but the use of the very strongest types of carbonfibre for the construction of their monocoques has paid off as they can now withstand impacts at speeds of up to 240mph, something of which their antecedents could only have dreamed.

Consider too the way in which the drivers of today go out to compete. A driver of the 1950s might have thought of them as spacemen. Indeed, the racer's uniform has changed out of all recognition. Look back to the 1950s, and many single-seater drivers wore cloth hats rather than helmets. Their cars pushed out 500bhp and could hit 180mph, but many Formula 1 drivers of the day even went out to battle wearing a short-sleeved cotton shirt so that they could keep cool when the races were long and summer was at its height. It was only when the single-seaters of the day followed the route of fitting the engine behind the driver rather than in front that cars started to be fitted with a roll hoop behind the driver's head to offer some form of protection should the car end up inverted. Furthermore, it wasn't until the middle of the following decade that all drivers accepted that wearing a safety harness might be a good idea. Indeed, with fire a terrible spectre for all, something that killed just as many as a severe impact, many preferred to be thrown clear in an impact than remain trapped on board and risk being burned to death.

Staying firmly in place in the case of an accident, strapped securely into a tailor-made seat wearing three-layer fireproof overalls that can withstand a full blaze for several minutes and a neckbrace to prevent whiplash injuries is now the accepted way to remain safe. Race and rally fans the world over must be thankful that such advances have been made so that we can watch the sport we love without the fear that the spectacular need end in tragedy.

Certainly, egos may be bruised, the drivers shaken and their budgets battered in an accident, but what is important is that we can marvel at the thrills and spills yet all say "and they walked away..." as the dust settles, the wrecked cars are cleared away and the racing recommences.

This book is dedicated to those moments when a driver overestimates their own ability and oversteps the mark, often with inevitable consequences, or is caught up in a moment caused by someone else doing the same and collecting them. A momentary loss of concentration is all it takes, a slippery patch of oil that they fail to notice or, perhaps, mechanical faliure. Indeed, some of the most spectacular accidents have happened when the car has cried 'enough', its suspension sagged or its brakes failed, leaving the driver incapable of doing anything but attempting to scrub off some speed by spinning the car or, if this isn't possible, taking their hands off the steering wheel, their feet off the pedals and crossing their arms across their chest to stop them flapping around in the ensuing moment and then saying their prayers.

Driver error happens at every level of the sport from World Champions to novice racers and from Grand Prix circuit to NASCAR oval to rally stage. As the level of racing category rises, so does the pressure to succeed and thus, as you would expect, there's usually a variance in opinion as to who caused any particular accident. However, there are also some extremely funny and even bizarre quotes from the drivers involved as they look back on moments that left them angry, embarrassed, battered, relieved or even proud.

So sit back, strap up and hold on for a bumpy ride as we take a ride through some of the most spectacular accidents of the the past four decades in which we can revel at their flights through the air, into the wall or onto their roof, always safe in the knowledge that they crashed but walked away...

Bruce Jones, London, 2004

"I saw it on TV after the race, and it looked quite exciting, but I didn't have any doubts about getting back in the car..."

Alexander Wu[

Canadian GP, Montreal, June 1998: Picture the scene. It's your first full year of Formula 1, you're driving for Benetton and you're 11th on the grid. Gallingly, your team-mate Giancarlo Fisichella is fourth. So it's obvious that you have even more reason than normal to plant your throttle foot and make up ground at the start. The dash to the first corner is short, the track narrowing into a tight left-hander that feeds almost immediately into a long right. To stand a chance of scoring points, it's imperative to pick off a few cars in the first few seconds. This is what Alexander Wurz was looking to do when something happened ahead of him. In F1, things happen so fast that there's seldom time to respond and, in an instant, Wurz was upside down bouncing across the gravel...

THINGS GO FROM BAD TO WURZ
FOR ALEX

001> WURZ

002> WURZ

005> WURZ

006> WURZ

What had happened was that Jacques Villeneuve had locked up and his Williams team-mate Heinz-Harald Frentzen had backed off to avoid him, catching out Jean Alesi behind him. As shown in photo 1, Wurz had to take to the grass but still clipped Alesi's Sauber and got airborne. Fortune favoured Frentzen as Wurz just missed him (photo 2), then slid across the track, starting to turn over (3) as Alesi's damaged car followed him, with Jarno Trulli's Prost also running out of room as Eddie Irvine threads his Ferrari through behind. On hitting the gravel bed, Wurz's Benetton dug in and started to roll (4). With wheels bouncing everywhere and Damon Hill keeping out ot trouble in the background, Trulli inspects the underside of Wurz's car (5) as it bounces past (6). The Italian then heaves a sigh of relief as the Benetton comes in to land in front of him rather than on him (7). Finally, with Alesi's team mate Johnny Herbert also beached in the gravel, having been pushed wide in the melee behind, Wurz comes to a halt (8), still calm despite rolling three times. The Austrian then ran back to the pits and took the spare car for the restart...

003> WURZ

004> WURZ

007> WURZ

008> WURZ

"As we went into the first corner I saw Wurz's car in the air above me. Fortunately, I was able to quickly change direction, otherwise for sure he would have landed on top of me"

Jarno Trulli

CLUB SOCIAL

50

CLUB SOCIAL CLUB SOCIAL

100

> 001> FIRMAN

> 002> FIRMAN

> 003> FIRMAN

> 007> FIRMAN

"I had a suspension failure that pitched me off the track at Turn 1"

Ralph Firman

FREEWHEELING FIRMAN

Brazilian GP, Interlagos, April 2003: Being in the driving seat suggests being in control. But we all know that this isn't always the case, as displayed here by Jordan racer Ralph Firman who proves that it's possible to be in the driving seat yet still be a passenger... This scary incident occurred when rain hit Brazil's annual bonanza and caused chaos. Unlike reigning World Champion Michael Schumacher and several others, Ralph didn't lose control through the river of water running across the track after the Senna S. No, he lost it on the start/finish straight. As you can see in this sequence of photos, though, it was absolutely not his fault. It would have been hard enough seeing through the spray kicked up by Olivier Panis and his own team-mate Giancarlo Fisichella, but to then find your view blocked by a wheel, one of your wheels, would have added somewhat to the situation. Pitching the car into a slide was the best solution to slowing his yellow rocket down, but avoiding an unsighted Panis was obviously not in question. Still, it could have been worse: he could have taken out his team-mate, that same team-mate who went on to win the race... Now you understand why success in motor racing is a bit of a lottery.

004> FIRMAN

005> FIRMAN

006> FIRMAN

008> FIRMAN

IT TAKES TWO TO TANGLE

Canadian GP, Montreal, June 1998: Staying calm after an accident is crucial, with the ability to steady your nerves and concentrate on the race ahead truly imperative. So, just half an hour after Alexander Wurz's race-stopping rolls on pages 12-15, it was time to do it all over again. Amazingly, lightning does strike twice, as Jarno Trulli and Jean Alesi experienced, both finding themselves removed from the running by the first corner. This time, Ralf Schumacher triggered the incident, his Jordan getting out of line and then spinning, bunching up those behind as they took evasive action. When the dust settled, Trulli's Prost was found sitting across the nose of Alesi's Sauber, its left rear wheel very close to the French driver's head. He was less than amused.

SPA'ING PARTNERS

Belgian GP, Spa-Francorchamps, August 1998: This was the year that Mika Hakkinen claimed the first of his two Formula 1 titles, but not everything went right for the Finn and McLaren. There had already been an aborted attempt to start the race, with 12 of the 22 cars being involved. With all but four of these patched up for a restart, pole starter Hakkinen was jumped by Damon Hill's Jordan on the run to the La Source hairpin. This is when things got too hot to handle on the wet track as chief title rival Michael Schumacher turned his Ferrari across his bows and they locked wheels. This tipped Hakkinen into a spin and, with no space in which to avoid him, he was collected by Johnny Herbert's Sauber. When weather conditions worsened, perhaps he didn't feel so bad watching from the sidelines, especially when Schumacher, unsighted in the spray, ploughed into the rear of Coulthard's car and also left the meeting without scoring.

> **"Hakkinen tried to put Michael off and made no attempt to run tight at the first corner. He tried to squeeze Michael against the pit wall"**
>
> Ferrari's Ross Brawn

EVEN SCHUEY
GETS 'TYRED'

Belgian GP, Spa-Francorchamps, August 1996: Even the best can get it wrong occasionally. Michael Schumacher had arrived at Ferrari as a double World Champion, but the chassis was not the best. In trying to make up for its shortcomings, the German genius overstepped the mark in Friday practice, having his F310 snap away from him at the Fagnes left-hander. The tyre wall in front of the crash barrier absorbed some of the impact, but Schumacher still tore a muscle in his right leg on impact. Not that it stopped him from winning on the Sunday...

AN UP AND OVER FROM
DOWN UNDER

Australian GP, Melbourne, March 2002: Every Grand Prix driver dreams of getting their campaign off to a flying start, but Ralf Schumacher took this more literally than most in the first race of the 2002 World Championship. Apart from winning, the most important thing for a driver is to beat his team-mate and this Ralf had done, lining his Williams up third on the grid, with Juan Pablo Montoya's a second slower, back in sixth. So far so good. But then came the start of the race. This was likely to be the best chance to pass the two Ferraris lining up ahead of him. Ralf was going to use all the horsepower available from his BMW engine and try to thread his way past the two red cars in front of him. Yet, as the title of this book suggests, things didn't go quite according to plan as Ralf and rival Rubens Barrichello came together for a truly hair-raising moment that guaranteed that the opening race of the season was given even more television airtime than normal and photographs of its wildest moment guaranteed more newsprint than normal. And, oh yes, they really did walk away. Ran, actually, in the preconditioned way that drivers have when they think that they might be able to take the team's spare car for the restart...

"Rubens Barrichello definitely changed direction on the road twice and we're only allowed to do it once"

Ralf Schumacher

> 001> AUSTRALIA

> 002> AUSTRA

> 005> AUSTRALIA

> 006> AUSTRAL

When is a swerve not a swerve? Observe how Rubens Barrichello leads away (1) with Michael Schumacher heading to the right of the photo. Ralf Schumacher makes a run up the middle (3) then Barrichello spots him (4). He starts to head him off (5), but as he moves to his left he takes the track that Ralf wanted. They clash and the Williams is sent skywards (6). Emphasising his greater pace, Ralf takes off the Ferrari's rear wing and keeps on rising (7). But what goes up must come down and Ralf slams down onto the grass (10) and then into the gravel, lucky to emerge unscathed.

> 009> AUSTRALIA

"Ralf says I braked early, but if I hadn't been there he would not have made the corner"

Rubens Barrichello

> 003> AUSTRALIA

> 004> AUSTRALIA

> 007> AUSTRALIA

> 008> AUSTRALIA

> 010> AUSTRALIA

> 011> AUSTRALIA

Austrian GP, the A1-Ring, May 2002: There are accidents and there are *accidents*. This one was so violent in its impact that it left even the most hard-nosed of onlookers deeply shocked. Yet, so strong are the Formula 1 cars of the 21st century that Takuma Sato, the driver of the exploding Jordan shown here, was talking of being fit and ready for the very next race a fortnight later. Had this shunt happened even as recently as the 1970s, he would not have lived... As it was, the cockpit of his Jordan was shattered but it had absorbed sufficient energy that the Japanese driver escaped with no more than bruising. Bruising almost from top to toe, admittedly. No shunt for years has exemplified the strength of an F1 car so well.

Sato was taken out by the spinning Sauber of Nick Heidfeld. He'd been negotiating Turn 2 - the uphill right-hander at the top of the hill - when Heidfeld lost control under braking on the entry to the corner and slammed gearbox first into the Jordan as it exited the turn. When the dust settled, Sato could see the ground through the remains of his cockpit and his legs were trapped, but he'd just survived one of the biggest smashes in F1 history.

BREAKIN' UP
ISN'T SO HARD TO DO

> 001> SATO

> 002> SATO

> 003> SATO

> 004> SATO

> 005> SATO

004> BRUNDLE

> 001> BRUNDLE

"There was something about a 'long' brake pedal and he thinks maybe his heel dabbed the throttle"

Tyrrell's Maurice Phillippe

AND BRUNDLE'S GOT HIS NOSE IN FRONT!

Monaco GP, Monaco, May 1984: Fresh out of Formula 3 and aware that the best place to impress would be on the streets of Monaco, Martin Brundle made an impact in his Tyrrell. Trouble was, it was the wrong sort of impact. It didn't half bring him to the attention of the world's media,though, even if the TV cameraman in the background was so busy watching the accident unfold that he forgot to point his camera at it... The spectacular upending came in the closing moments of qualifying at Tabac, the fast left-hander on the harbourfront before Piscine. Martin entered the corner just a fraction too fast, but the impact with the barriers still ripped the wheels off the left side of his car before he slid along the track, hearing the rasp of metal on tarmac. You can be sure that when he clambered out and removed his helmet that he would have had to endure ribald comments from those aboard the yachts in the harbour on how they could have done better... The photographers separated from the accident by the thickness of the crash barrier probably took rather longer to regain the power of speech.

IF YOU CAN'T STAND THE HEAT...

German GP, Hockenheim, July 1994: Fire was all too commonplace in the 1950s and 1960s. World Champion Niki Lauda nearly perished in it in 1976, but it had become mercifully rare after that, which is why motorsport fans were rocked on their heels when this inflagration engulfed the Benetton pitcrew in 1994. What triggered it was a faulty valve in one of the team's refuelling nozzles when its number two driver Jos Verstappen dropped in for a tank full of fuel and four new tyres. A drop of fuel hit his car's hot engine and ignited, instantly enveloping those around in a ball of flame. Quick work with extinguishers by the attendant mechanics on fire watch duty brought the situation under control, but not before two mechanics' overalls had caught fire. Verstappen simply closed his visor, found his belt buckle, popped it and, amid a ball of flame, clambered out. Unsurprisingly, there were calls for refuelling to be banned, but some said that this was just a case of people getting a little hot under the collar, albeit nothing like as hot as this mechanic...

"I thought that it was water on my visor, but there was a fireball Luckily, it was all over in a few seconds but it seemed like an hour"

Jos Verstappen

ARNOUX
TAKES ON TARZAN

Dutch GP, Zandvoort, July 1982: Nestling in the sand dunes on Holland's North Sea coast, the Zandvoort circuit is little more than a stone's throw from the beach. And this is where Renault's Rene Arnoux appeared to be heading when he went straight on at the Tarzan corner. What this photo sequence of him slamming into, then up and over the tyre wall before coming to rest on top of it and the crash barrier that it was protecting shows, is that his offside front wheel had parted company with the car just when he needed it most as he braked for the 180-degree right-hander at the end of the unusually long start/finish straight. "When the wheel came off, I had no steering and no brakes... I just waited for the impact," explained Rene. Despite having started from pole position, Rene had fallen to fourth place a few laps before the accident and recalled later that he had felt a vibration for several laps but had assumed that it was tyre wear. So, when people say that some drivers have mechanical sympathy, please be aware that this doesn't mean that all do...

> 004> ARNOUX

> 005> ARNOUX

"I saw a car go sideways, then hit me in the back and go over the top of me. I didn't know who it was"

Jarno Trulli

Formula 1 testing, Valencia, May 2000: Accidents will happen, but nothing riles a driver more than being involved in a big one if he feels that it was either unnecessary or, worse still, caused by someone else or, worst of all, both... This is one such and it occurred not in a race but in testing, making the contact between the two cars all the harder to understand. It's not as though they would have been racing for position. Still, Fisichella slammed his Benetton into Trulli's Jordan at the Turn 11 hairpin, taking off its rear wing as he somersaulted clean over the top before landing nose first in a gravel trap and bouncing over once more and coming to rest, fortunately, the right way up. "It was really crazy," exclaimed Trulli. "He made a really big mistake. I was on my installation lap and I saw a car coming up behind me and moved over to let it by. Then I saw it go sideways, hit me in the back and fly over the top of me. I didn't know who it was." To add insult to injury, this was their second clash in four days, the first coming in the European GP. It was clearly time for these compatriots to sit down and clear the air before meeting on a race track again.

FISICHELLA FLIPS OUT

001> FISCHELLA

002> FISCHEL

005> FISCHELLA

006> FISCHEL

009> FISCHELLA

010> FISCHEL

003> FISCHELLA

004> FISCHELLA

007> FISCHELLA

008> FISCHELLA

011> FISCHELLA

012> FISCHELLA

"BABY BEAR" SPILLS HIS PORRIDGE...

British GP, Silverstone, July 1973: This is one of the most famous crashes in F1 history, in which a keen rookie tried to impress and did quite the opposite. The driver in question is Jody Scheckter, driving a third McLaren. The result was the race being stopped after his spin out at Woodcote led to mayhem, taking out eight cars. Team-mate Denny "The Bear" Hulme summed it up best: "Baby Bear [Jody] didn't need any help to spill his porridge. From where I was sitting – about two lengths behind him at 135mph through Woodcote – it looked as though there was going to be porridge and broken chairs all over the place."

"The first thing that I saw was the wheel in the air. After that I was flying sideways"

Formula 1 testing, Silverstone, April 2000: Some drivers have all the luck while others seem to be tripped up throughout their career. Brazil's Ricardo Zonta, while talented enough to win the Formula 3000 title, falls into the latter camp. He'd endured two huge accidents when racing for BAR in the team's first season in 1999, but they were dwarfed by what he experienced when testing in 2000. Hammering down the Hangar Straight towards Stowe at 190mph, he hit a problem : his suspension broke, and his car snapped into a spin. It bounced over the gravel trap, hit the tyre wall side on and then cleared the barriers and, worryingly, the debris fencing too. But, once again, he walked away...

HORI-ZONTA-L.
RICARDO ZONTA PROVES CARS CAN FLY

> **001>** GERMANY 2000

> **002>** GERMANY 2000

> **003>** GERMANY 200

GERMANY TAKE 1: 2000
HOW NOT TO DO IT

> **005>** GERMANY 200C

> **009>** GERMANY 2000

> **010>** GERMANY 200

German GP, Hockenheim, July 2000: Even the very best get it wrong from time to time, as Michael Schumacher demonstrated in his home race. Still gunning for his first driver title with Ferrari and with McLaren's David Coulthard and Mika Hakkinen right with him on points, he was anxious to bounce back after two straight retirements. But this was not the way to do it... His first mistake was to make a bad start, but this was made worse by Hakkinen sweeping past. Running down to the first corner, hoping at least to slot into third place, Michael's Ferrari ran out towards the outside edge of the circuit, leaving Giancarlo Fisichella nowhere to go in his Benetton. He locked up but they clashed and, for once, took out only themselves as they bounced through the gravel trap into the barriers. Fearing that Michael had lost his bearings, a helpful marshal offers the fallen hero directions back to the pits.

"We're racing in a hard and fair way.
We're not happy families out for a drive"

Michael Schumacher

> 004> GERMANY 2000

> 006> GERMANY 2000

> 007> GERMANY 2000

> 008> GERMANY 2000

"When I saw him it was too late to avoid the crash. The accident looked worse on TV than it did in the car"

Luciano Burti

GERMANY TAKE 2: 2001
HERE WE GO AGAIN!

German GP, Hockenheim, July 2001: Spectators who enjoyed the thrills and spills of the first corner of the 2000 German GP would have made sure they had seats in the grandstands overlooking this stretch of track for 2001. And they would not have been disappointed, for this was considerably more impressive. Michael Schumacher was involved again, but it was Prost driver Luciano Burti who caught everybody's attention. And how! When the lights went out to get the race underway, Michael's home race curse struck again as gearchange gremlins hit his Ferrari. Sitting stationary at the head of a charging pack is never a good place to be... And his luck ran out when Luciano slammed into his rear. Prost then rocketed skywards before landing tail first almost on top of Enrique Bernoldi's Arrows and then barrel rolling along the track into the gravel trap. The pair walked back towards the pits, but then Michael noticed that the race was being stopped and, realising that this meant that he could take the spare car, immediately started sprinting back to his pit. A World Champion, you see, always has his eyes open.

Argentinian GP, Buenos Aires, April 1996: Some races run without missing a beat, but also without producing a single moment of drama. Others seem to throw action at you from every angle. This was one of them. Luca Badoer clipped Pedro Diniz's Ligier with his Forti and went a-rolling. Unfortunately for the Italian, it came to a halt upside down, leaving him to remember not to simply pop his belts to get out, as that would have led to him falling downwards onto his head. You may laugh, but this has happened more times than is funny as drivers race to get away from their inverted wrecks. Then, five laps later, Diniz roared back on track after a pitstop, only for his filler nozzle not to have closed, allowing petrol to slosh out when he braked for the first time and ignite on the hot engine. It made for quite a fireball and gave the Brazilian a chance to show just how quickly he could evacuate his car... A few laps later, Tarso Marques kept the action coming thick and fast when he slammed his Minardi into Martin Brundle's Jordan, taking both out.

ARGY BARGY!

> 001> ARGENTINA '96

> 002> ARGENTINA '96

> 003> ARGENTINA '96

> 004> ARGENTINA '96

UPSIDE DOWN YOU TURN ME!

Portuguese GP, Estoril, September 1989: Roberto Moreno was one of those drivers for whom the breaks never came. Driving for Coloni wasn't seen as a way forward. Indeed, Roberto found great difficulty going forward as this sequence shows. He was flat-out in qualifying when he came across Eddie Cheever's Arrows at Turn 3 and then his rodeo ride began. He was fortunate not to roll, but still hit the barriers hard. The penalty, though was mental anguish rather than physical pain.

"...EXCUSE ME, I THINK THERE'S A CAR ON MY HEAD"

Mexican GP, Mexico City, June 1991: A little bravery can go a long way, but a lot can get you into trouble as reigning World Champion Ayrton Senna found out when he attempted to take the circuit's toughest corner, Peraltada, in sixth gear. To make matters worse, just as he moved his hand to the gear lever to change up from fifth the car hit one of the many bumps and snapped away from him, whipping into a 180 degree spin before hitting the tyre wall and flipping over. And to think that this happened just a few days after he was hit on the head by a jet ski...His stars were clearly very much out of alignment.

"HOLD IT THERE, I'LL BE RIGHT BACK!"

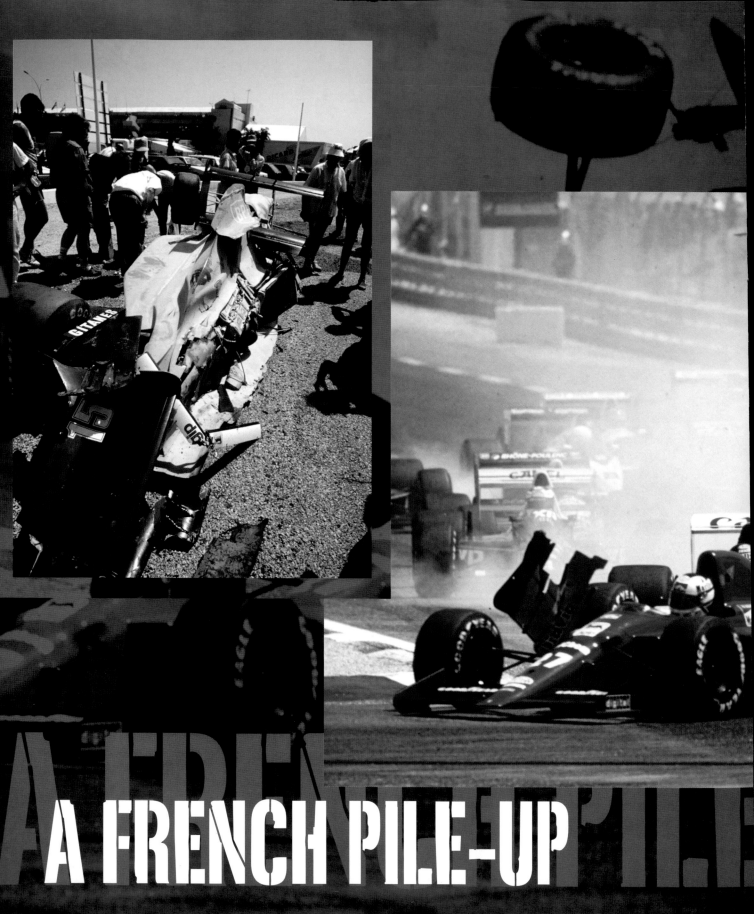

A FRENCH PILE-UP

"I aimed for a gap, but suddenly there was Mansell right in front, Berger to the left and Boutsen to the right"

Mauricio Gugelmin

French GP, Paul Ricard, July 1989: Motor racing can be bright, colourful, loud and spectacular. That's what it says on the tin, and that's what it delivered here. This vibrant accident had the lot, with star performer Mauricio Gugelmin scoring big for artistic merit. Alain Prost went on to win the race but, afterwards, few could talk about anything other than this first corner accident. It was really, rather special. Gugelmin had started from 10th place and had clear ambitions to make up places at the start. But then

so did every other driver out there. "I aimed for a gap," he would say later, "but suddenly there was Mansell right in front, Berger to the left and Boutsen to the right. As the gap closed, I braked a little harder, locked my front wheels and that was it..." The next thing that anyone knew, there was an explosion of car parts, with Gugelmin's March silhouetted against the sky after using Nigel Mansell's Ferrari as a launch pad. The Brazilian's March was junked but Gugelmin simply took the restart in the spare...

> 001> FRANCE '89

> 002> FRANC

> 005> FRANCE '89

> 006> FRANCE

> 009> FRANCE '89

> 010> FRANCE

"Something comes out of the air and slams into me. It gave me a belt and for a while I couldn't see very much"

Nigel Mansell

> 003> FRANCE '89

> 004> FRANCE '89

> 007> FRANCE '89

> 008> FRANCE '89

> 011> FRANCE '89

Brazilian GP, Interlagos, April 2003: Many describe an F1 monocoque as a survival cell and this has seldom been more obvious than when Mark Webber rattled his Jaguar off the walls enclosing the track to bring this race to an early finish. Bashed and battered from the impacts, he came to a halt sitting in a cockpit from which all four wheels and suspension had been ripped. Oh, and nose cone, nose wings, barge boards, turning vanes and much more besides. There was so much debris littering the track that the organisers had no choice but to send out the safety car for a record fifth time, but when Fernando Alonso failed to observe the yellow flags and arrived at the crash scene at 180mph, only to hit it and slam his Renault into the wall, there was no choice but to call a halt to proceedings... Webber and Alonso weren't alone in leaving red-faced as Juan Pablo Montoya, Michael Schumacher, Jenson Button and Jos Verstappen went off at Turn 3. The FIA was red-faced too, as it got confused with its own rules on countback and awarded victory to Kimi Raikkonen, only to have to give it to Giancarlo Fisichella at a later date.

WEBBER'S WHEELS

Uninjured but embarrassed, Mark Webber comes to a halt, his broken and steaming Jaguar no longer blessed with wheels with which to drive or steer... All he'd done was drift off line to cool his tyres, but he lost control

Jarno Trulli manages to do what his Renault team-mate Fernando Alonso failed to do and picks his way past the debris strewn across the track at the beginning of the start/finish straight by Mark Webber's accident

DINIZ GOES OFF-ROADING

001> DINIZ

002> DINIZ

003> DIN

007> DINIZ

008> DINIZ

009> DIN

European GP, the Nurburgring, September 1999: Inverting a modern racing car is always going to come as a surprise to the driver, but they can usually rely on their head and shoulders being protected by the roll hoop, especially in a modern day F1 car. But not always, as Pedro Diniz discovered when Alexander Wurz pitched his Sauber into a roll and found the ground to be closer to his helmet than it should have been as the roll hoop sheared when the car slid over a kerb. Luckily, Sauber had long championed high cockpit sides and these kept him from ending up rather shorter than he'd been at the outset...

"I saw Pedro fly passed me and was worried as I was on the scene when they were tending to him"

Damon Hill

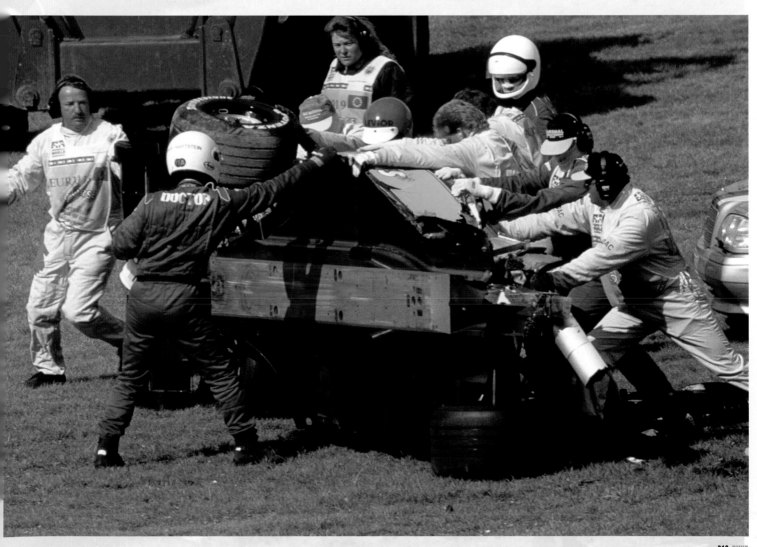

SAY YOUR DALY PRAYERS

Monaco GP, Monaco, May 1980: The first corner of any Grand Prix is where most accidents happen and especially at Monaco. Not only is it incredibly tight, but the rest of the circuit is so narrow that it's all but impossible to overtake anywhere else, making the pressure to pass here even greater than usual. Ste Devote is where the drivers hold their breath and brake as late as they dare. Trouble is, some like Derek Daly leave it that little bit too late. This photo shows his Tyrrell taking a rather different line to everyone else. He'd hit Bruno Giacomelli's Alfa Romeo, clipped Alain Prost's McLaren and come back down on top of Jean-Pierre Jarier. Yes, he took out his team-mate... Daly said: "I remember that afterwards Jean-Pierre was saying to Bruno 'you hit me'. Bruno said that he hadn't and Alain hadn't a clue what was going on. Then Jean-Marie Balestre waded in and told everyone that I was responsible." Then, after a short walk back to the pits, Derek not only made his excuses to team owner Ken Tyrrell but also apologised to his mechanics whose work load he'd just increased, big time.

British GP, Brands Hatch, July 1976: F1 fans have long missed the thrills provided by Brands Hatch, with its bowl-like terrain affording great viewing. Best of its corners was Paddock Hill Bend and it was here that the race burst into life on its opening lap. Niki Lauda led away from pole and Ferrari was delighted as team-mate Clay Regazzoni demoted Lauda's chief rival James Hunt to third. But Regazzoni clipped Lauda and started to spin. Hunt had nowhere to go and his McLaren bounced off Regazzoni onto two wheels before slamming back to earth, scattering those behind. The race was stopped, but when it became clear that it would be restarted without Hunt the crowd went wild and refused to shut up until he was readmitted. He went on to win but the sport's governing body later disqualified him and gave the race win to Lauda.

STILL IN THE HUNT

EDDIE THINKS DAMON'S OVER THE HILL.

Portuguese GP, Estoril, September 1994: One glance at the photograph above gives you more than a clue that one of these drivers has got this corner somewhat wrong. We'll give you a clue: despite having all four wheels off the deck, it's not Damon Hill's Williams on the left. No, it's Eddie Irvine's Jordan on the right. He'd spun at the circuit's new chicane and left Damon with nowhere to go as he arrived in maximum attack mode on a qualifying lap. "What can you do?" asked Damon philosophically. "Eddie lost control. He didn't do it deliberately. I could see him coming back across the track, but there was nowhere to go. It was the first time that I've been upside down in a racing car. It may have looked pretty tame on television, but there's still 500kg of racing car on top of you..."

RAIN NEEDED IN SPAIN...

Spanish GP, Jarama, April 1970: The mere thought of fire still makes drivers of the 1950s and 1960s break into a cold sweat. This charred aftermath shows that fire was still a threat in the 1970s. Indeed, it took a great deal of bravery from a spectating soldier to pull Jacky Ickx from the wreckage of his flaming Ferrari. He and Jackie Oliver had been fighting over fifth place on the opening lap when the BRM's brakes failed and Oliver tried to aim his car off the circuit past Ickx but slammed amidships into the Ferrari. Fuel tanks still erupted in those days and this happened in a flash. Ickx's overalls were ablaze as he struggled to release a bent belt buckle to free himself, and was pulled clear to be doused by the marshals. Trouble was, he was left in his fuel-soaked overalls and suffered second degree burns all over. Worse still, the marshals allowed his burning car roll back across the track, leaving a wall of burning fuel in its wake. Still, at least Ickx walked away...

NASCAR Winston Cup, Chicagoland, July 2003: Terry Labonte found himself a little warmer than he'd have liked when an accident unfolded in front of him and, in the flash of an eye, he was part of it. Casey Mears and Johnny Benson had collided and Benson's car bounced right into the path of Labonte's Joe Gibbs Racing Chevrolet Monte Carlo. Labonte hit him and spun up the banking. Straight into the wall. And it was this impact that ripped the rear off his car and crushed the fuel cell, leading to this oh so spectacular flame-out. It was ime to get out of there, but first Labonte had to wait for his blazing wreck to come to a halt, praying that no one would hit him.

FLAMING
LABONTE

> 001> LABONTE

> 002> LABONTE

> 003> LABON

> 006> LABONTE

> 007> LABON

> 009> LABONTE

> 010> LABON

"It looked worse than it was. I smell like a barbecue. Other than that I feel fine"

Terry Labonte

Labonte's Chevrolet kept on sliding along the wall, a terrible screeching of metal on concrete filling his ears as the acrid smell of burning filled his nostrils. Then, once the car had drifted down to the grassy infield, Labonte started to evacuate, popping his belt and posting himself out of the window as fast as he could as the inferno raged away at the rear of the car. The fire tender was soon on the scene to douse both driver and car. "It looked worse than it was," he told reporters. "I smell like a barbecue, but other than that I feel fine."

NASCAR Winston Cup, Daytona 500, February 2003: No racing series has as many high-speed or multi-car smashes as NASCAR's premier stock car racing formula. This example from 2003 is typical of what happens when you fill a banked oval with more than 40 hard-charging heavyweight cars running in close company. One steals the air off the nose of the car behind and this is what happens. Mayhem hardly covers it as war breaks out and everyone behind has to act, quickly... The conundrum is whether to try to avoid a spinning car or to aim at where it is now, on the basis that it ought to have moved elsewhere in the fraction of a second before you reach it. On the other hand...

This squeeze with Ward Burton and Ken Schrader, subsequent wall slam, slide down the banking into the infield and aerial bouncing sequence is what befell Ryan Newman in NASCAR's big one: the Daytona 500. But then his battered Penske Racing Dodge Intrepid dug in when it reached the grass infield and was pitched into a spectacular series of rolls that went on and on and on. It really wasn't the ideal way to launch his 2003 campaign.

NUKED NEWMAN 1

"I was just in the wrong place at the wrong time. We came off the last turn three-wide and I got hit"

Ryan Newman

003> NEWMAN1

002> NEWMAN1

"... and then I was pointing towards the wall. It was a pretty hard hit..." **Ryan Newman**

So, there he was giving his car a rattling ride across the grass of the infield when Ryan Newman thought that he'd offer keen model makers a chance to take a look at the underside of his car, to help them with their detailing. "Aah, so that's how the exhaust pipe is ducted," they must have been thinking as they trained their binoculars on the flipping Dodge from the safety of their seats high in the massive grandstands...

004> NEWMAN1

005> NEWMA

008> NEWMAN1

009>NEWMAN

012> NEWMAN1

013> NEWMAN1

"... and when I saw the grass I figured that I was in more trouble than hitting the wall"

Ryan Newman

006> NEWMAN1

007> NEWMAN1

010> NEWMAN1

011> NEWMAN1

014> NEWMAN1

015> NEWMAN1

Not content with entertaining the fans with a solitary flip, Ryan kept the momentum going and threw in four more for good effect. What's impressive, apart from this dedicated showmanship, is the way that the Dodge held together through its violent passage, with its roll cage doing its job well so that the fast arriving safety workers were able to look in, check Ryan was alright and then extract him. The car, however, was never to race again.

BATTLE OF THE BANKING

NASCAR Busch Series, Bristol, August 2001: Larry Foyt slides sideways up by the wall, after a collision with Michael Waltrip as Kevin Lepage thanks his lucky stars that he was running lower down the narrow Bristol banking, emphasising how it can be a something of a lottery competing on short ovals.

NASCAR Busch Series, Bristol, August 2001: Seeing where you're going is a great help when you're travelling at 150mph, as Ron Hornaday Jr. discovers as he's faced with a wall of tyre smoke thrown up by a sideways car right in his path. Judging by the nose of his car, he knows it's there... He might even have tipped it into a spin in the first place. And if he found the view poor, think what the driver to his right must have thought. With zero visibility, he'd have had to steer his car by smell or sixth sense

OVER
BLOWN...

NASCAR Winston Cup, Dover International Speedway, September 2003: Emphasising how all best laid plans can come undone by elements beyond a driver's control, Joe Nemechek finds his race is run when he climbs from his battered and reshaped Chevrolet Monte Carlo after one of his tyres suffered a blow-out and sent him spinning into the wall.

SADLER UP

NASCAR Winston Cup, Kansas Speedway, October 2003: The race was 400 miles long, but not everybody managed to keep their cars off the wall for all of that time, with Elliott Sadler having a wretched time as his Chevrolet rattled along the concrete and then caught fire. Finding that he was unable to get out of the car unaided, it's not surprising that he was feeling the worse for wear when he was helped out of the car by the safety crew. Sadler called for cars to be fitted with roof hatches to make it easier to get out after an accident.

"**I couldn't get out of the car like I wanted to. The hatch can't come soon enough**" Elliott Sadler

NEW HAMPSHIRE
NIGHTMARE

NASCAR Winston Cup, New Hampshire International Speedway, July 2001: It's that man Joe Nemechek again, this time taking an unusual approach to proceedings by driving backwards into the NHIS retaining wall. And, as on the page opposite, Elliott Sadler is in on the action. Everyone else elected to stick with what they knew best: the safety of running on the circuit's only racing line, low on the track.

LOOK OUT: IT'S BEHIND YOU!

NASCAR Busch Grand National, Dover International Speedway, September 2000: Fire at the back, fire at the front then then fire at the back again, Mike Skinner's Chevrolet Monte Carlo leaves a trail of burning fuel as he gyrates down off the banking to the apron, seeking a place out of harm's way where he can park up near a fire tender and get the heck out of there. And fast...

SMOKIN'!

NASCAR Winston Cup, Atlanta Motor Speedway, March 2001: Jerry Nadeau spins as Buckshot Jones (44) holds his breath and squeezes by in his Petty Enterprises Dodge Intrepid. However, while spinning is one thing, finishing is quite another and although there's a saying that "spinners aren't winners", they can be finishers and Nadeau somehow kept his Hendrick Motorsports Chevrolet Monte Carlo off the wall during this spin to motor on and avoid all further mishaps to finish the race in third place.

"While spinning is one thing, finishing is quite another, although there is a saying that spinners aren't winners"

FROM POLE TO WALL.

NASCAR Winston Cup, Daytona 500, February 2003: Jeff Green was delighted when he qualified on pole. But he wasn't smiling any more when he modified the tail of his Chevrolet against the wall at Turn 4 after a clash with Jimmy Spencer. Note the pair of roof flaps that are fitted to rise and help to slow the car if it's running backwards.

"I blew a right rear tyre, right in the middle of the corner. I guess it just wasn't meant to be"

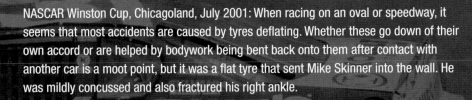

NASCAR Winston Cup, Chicagoland, July 2001: When racing on an oval or speedway, it seems that most accidents are caused by tyres deflating. Whether these go down of their own accord or are helped by bodywork being bent back onto them after contact with another car is a moot point, but it was a flat tyre that sent Mike Skinner into the wall. He was mildly concussed and also fractured his right ankle.

SPINNER SKINNER

SMOKY SHUNT

NASCAR Winston Cup, Talladega Superspeedway, April 2000: This is the fastest track on the calendar, so they didn't name this race the DieHard 500 for nothing and all the big guns are involved in this smoky mix-up. There's Michael Waltrip (7) on the left of frame facing backwards and Robby Gordon spinning down the banking as Robert Pressley (77) and Stacy Compton (9) desperately try to stay low on the track to keep out of the way. All told, fully 16 of the 43-car field became involved, perhaps explaining how Jeff Gordon was able to start 36th yet come through to win. The incident came three laps after the field was released following a caution, which explains why the cars were running in such close order and couldn't all avoid each other when Jeremy Mayfield triggered this chain reaction by bumping Scott Pruett who hit Robby Gordon before the others joined in.

HAVE A NICE WALTRIP

He left the race in a shower of sparks that were more spectacular than a fireworks display

NASCAR Winston Cup, Richmond International Speedway, September 2000: Some drivers really do love to be centre stage. Not content with his bit part in the massed crash on the opposite page, Michael Waltrip is at it again. This time it's a spectacular solo display, in which his Chevrolet Monte Carlo left the race in a shower of sparks that were more spectacular than a fireworks display but less enjoyable. Well, to him... Fittingly, the race was named The Chevrolet Monte Carlo 400. Just think what might have happened had he been driving a Pontiac earlier in the year when the race at Richmond three-quarter mile oval was named The Pontiac Excitement 400!

KRESTA RUN!

World Rally Championship, Rally Deutschland, July 2003: Racing drivers face risks at every turn, but they're nothing compared to those negotiated by rally drivers as they "give it death" on stages rather than on sanitised racing circuits. There are seldom barriers to contain their cars once they're on an unplanned trajectory. Indeed, they're just as likely to bend metal against a rock outcrop, a fence post or a tree, or even "get air" over the edge of a precipice. Danger lurks around every corner and it's up to the co-driver to call the pace notes accurately, and then up to the driver to decide just how hard he wants to attack. But still the rally drivers give it their all. Take this roll by Roman Kresta. He's clearly going for it just a little too much into this right-hander, especially as this wasn't in the event proper, just the shakedown. Some shakedown... The Peugeot privateer was limbering up to give it his best shot in the rally in the hope of impressing the works teams. As it happens, he didn't let this inversion affect him and was quickly "back on the horse" once the rally got underway and showing an equal amount of commitment but a superior level of skill as he was fastest on a stage for the first time.

>   002> KRESTA

>   003> KRESTA

004> FIRMAN

"Danger lurks around every corner and it's up to the co-driver to call the pace notes accurately"

McRAE
ROCKS AND ROLLS...

World Rally Championship, Cyprus Rally, April 2002: Colin McRae was the star of the early 1990s, the fastest but also the most spectacular rally driver in the world. Inevitably, there were accidents as he showed no fear as he took risk after risk, jumping his car higher than any rival would dare and cutting corners more than was really wise, but his speed was unrivalled.

> 001> MCRAE

"The mangled Ford came to rest back on its wheels and Colin did what all good rally drivers do, as if by instinct: he gunned the throttle"

Over the years, World Champion McRae eliminated most of the causes of accidents that littered his early career, but not all of them… Take this Focus-bending roll in Cyprus. It was his second. Not his second of the rally, but his second of the day… It wasn't a good day for the Ford team, as Colin clipped a concrete block early on and damaged his car's steering. Then team-mate Markko Martin inverted his Focus at the very same point, with Ford privateer Janne Tuohino coming within a whisker of doing the same… In this second roll, Colin carried plenty of speed into a fast corner but slid wide. This wouldn't have mattered if there hadn't been a muddy patch on the outside that caused his Focus to dig in and he was suddenly rolling onto his roof. But it didn't stop there and the car went over again, modifying the roofline at the rear. Fortunately, the mangled Ford came to rest back on its wheels and Colin did what all good rally drivers do, as if by instinct: he gunned the throttle. Sadly, he was disorientated and he headed off in the wrong direction before co-driver Nicky Grist made him do a u-turn. Then, at the end of the stage, Colin vented his anger by giving the car a good kicking…

> 003> SATO

> 004> SATO

> 005> SATO

"On Tarmac there's very little room for error, no chance to react"

MORE & MOREL

World Rally Championship, Tour de Corse, October, 2001: Car racing takes place almost invariably on tarmac, but rallying embraces every surface from ice and snow to gravel, to mud ... and to tarmac, the fastest surface of all. While tarmac offers the greatest levels of grip, with ice the least, it also means the greatest speeds and that, my friends, can spell the largest accidents. These occur in a flash when either the driver makes a mistake or the co-driver suggests, say, that a corner might be a fifth gear right when it's a third gear left. "On tarmac, there's very little room for error, no chance to react," explains former World Champion Richard Burns. "If something goes fractionally wrong then, bang, you're in the wall". The Tour de Corse is a tarmac rally. However, the reason that the drivers fear Corsica like nowhere else is because it's mountainous and its stages run along roads with rock faces on one side and precipices on the other, meaning that more than a little caution would be wise. Trouble is, few rally drivers can even spell the word. Privateer Fabrice Morel was fortunate that this accident happened in the foothills rather than the mountains, but he and co-driver David Marty still went on a journey that sent them 50 metres down into a ravine.

002> MOR

Where it all went wrong for Morel and Marty was at a fast right-hand bend. Coming in too fast, it was clear that they weren't going to make it and their little Peugeot was soon starting to turn turtle. The meagre grass verge couldn't stop them. And nor could the flimsy wire fence beyond. Then the French duo really came into their own as the roll was followed by a sequence of somersaults. Fortunately, they missed the trees at the corner and travelled over a hillside of scrub before crashing through a few saplings and coming to a halt at the bottom of the valley.

003>

"Corsica is particularly dangerous with unacceptable drops and a lack of protection by the side of the road

Colin McRae

Morel was slightly hurt, while Marty suffered back injuries. Strangely, it's almost always the co-driver who comes off worse. With Tommi Makinen also suffering a massive accident on the same event, his Mitsubishi ending up perched over a precipice, there were calls for the event to be dropped. Colin McRae was among them, saying: "Corsica is particularly dangerous with unacceptable drops and a lack of protection by the side of the road. One foot more and Tommi would have been dead."

> 004> MOREL

> 005> MOREL

World Rally Championship, Rally Deutschland, August 2002: Flying off a road is frightening. But flying off a road into trees is what really focuses a rally driver's attention. Ask Armin Schwarz... This spectacular bonding with nature occurred when his works Hyundai Accent, struggling with a punctured right rear tyre, slid wide through a fast right-hander on the Panzerplatte stage on the second morning of the three-day rally. Drivers always say that it goes horribly quiet when their cars leave the ground, with no tyre noise to speak of. But, as what goes up must come down, so there was soon a rending of metal as the Hyundai hit the trees at almost unabated speed, ripping open its left side. The car then bounced right and made further heavy impact with its right front corner. The strength of modern rally roll cages was shown by the fact that Schwarz and co-driver Manfred Hiemer came out of the wreck alive, but they were taken to hospital with a dislocated rib and heavy chest bruising respectively. This reinforced that tarmac rallies are fast and trees are solid, something that rally drivers would do well to remember.

TREE TOTAL.

> 001> ARGENTINA '96

> 005> ARGENTINA '96

CLUB RACING

One car gets in under another and propels it into the wall, something that happens a lot as the drivers dice for position

Midgets, Indiana State Fairground, September 2002: If ever there was a category of motor racing that was steeped in spectacular accidents, it is midget racing. Beloved for its close, entertaining racing action on America's quarter-mile ovals, it offers fans the sight of very small, very garish cars being driven very sideways, usually on dirt, their progress marked by a spray of dirt, sometimes a blaze of sparks and always by a wall of sound. They also crash a lot. No wonder the fans flock through the turnstiles to watch them.

The accident sequence shown here is typical of the all but inevitable midget incidents as one car gets in under another and propels it into the wall, something that happens a lot as the drivers dice for position at the entry of the corners. But where one goes, the others tend to follow, with many an end-over-end actually happening not to the car that was tipped off in the first case, but to one of the cars veering off course in avoidance...

MIDGETS GET MASHED!

UP ON THE ROOF

Formula 3, Blandford, August 1949: Major Peter Braid was the man in command in this famous accident when competing in his Formula 3 Cooper. You'd have thought that his military intelligence would have helped him know where he was going, especially as the circuit was laid out around an army camp.

As it was, he got it wrong, very wrong running over the crest at Engineers bend, the fastest corner on the circuit, ending up with his Cooper perched atop the roof of the guardroom, having hit a bus stop and a small tree between leaving the track and reaching his unintended destination.

With other accidents in the same meeting leaving one driver dead and another in hospital, leading motor racing journalist WB Boddy issued a stern but accurate conclusion to people who said that the Blandford circuit was too dangerous: "It's the racing driver's job to stay on the road. No one suggested that Monaco, for instance, was dangerous on account of its nature."

"It's the racing driver's job to stay on the road"

WB Boddy

001> DALZIEL

Formula Vauxhall, Knockhill, August 1999: Some of the whackiest racing accidents come in the junior categories, when drivers are learning their craft. Some learn from their mistakes, others don't. Well, not until their parents decide not to pay anymore…

FORMULA VIOLENCE

"I tried to shut the door on the inside. then I felt a bang at the back and Dalziel flew over me "

Iain Brown

002> DALZIEL

003> DALZI

006> DALZIEL

007> DALZIE

010> DALZIEL

Ryan Dalziel (8) arrived in his native Scotland as championship leader, but his hopes of shining on home turf came to naught on the opening lap when he got together with another local hero, Iain Brown (20). Not content with hitting Brown up the tail, Dalziel took off over him and pitched into a series of barrel rolls, giving eventual race winner Gary Paffett (16) quite a show as he rolled.

004> DALZIEL

005> DALZIEL

008> DALZIEL

009> DALZIEL

012> DALZIEL

HEADINGSOUTH

Formula Ford, Silverstone, June 1984: Formula Ford at Silverstone was always a mouth-watering prospect for those who liked their racing exciting. Well, any race in which cars run three-abreast into corners and then try to make that five-abreast is bound to grab your attention. Back in the early 1980s, it offered the most competitive racing on the planet as a host of future Formula 1 drivers cut their teeth in the sport.

This race was no different, but the star of this piece, Paul South, stuck his neck out just a little bit too far in his quest for glory. Trying to make space for himself into the notorious Woodcote chicane, something that was akin to trying to pass a camel through the eye of a needle, he clipped a rival's wheel and started a flight of which the Wright brothers would have been proud. Having started cartwheeling, he hit and cleared the tyre barrier and kept on bouncing, right towards a hospitality suite in which his sponsors were entertaining guests, no doubt hoping to get them to support Paul as well. Oh well!.

001> SOUTH

002> SOUTH

003> SOUTH

004> SOUTH

005> SOUTH

006> SOUTH

007> SOUTH

008> SOUTH

009>

010> SOUTH

"The cars are made to be equal which ensures that racing will be close"

RENAULT FUEGO

Renault Clios, Brands Hatch, June 2002: One-make racing is perpetually popular in club racing circles as it's cheap and the cars are made to be equal which ensures that racing will be close as no-one enjoys a mechanical advantage. Trouble is, this equality makes it hard to find the extra speed to pass the car ahead, which leads to drivers taking some major risks...

The fiery outcome of this accident involving Jason Templeman is not what the spectators had been waiting for, though. To make matters worse, he'd been tipped into a spin by Andrew Kirkaldy, then hit by Bob Smith, his own team-mate...

001> RENAULT

005> RENAU

005> RENAULT

006> RENAULT

007> RENAU

RENAULT

RENAULT

RENAULT

RENAULT

Formula Ford, Brands Hatch, October 2003: The Formula Ford Festival is an annual get-together of the world's best Formula Ford drivers. Unfortunately, some drivers take this a little too literally, as Indian driver Suk Sandher discovered when arrived at the Druids hairpin at the top of the hill. Just as he focused on getting his braking right, he experienced a helping hand from behind from Ollie Smith and, in an instant, was flipping over, bouncing on his roll hoop and heading off to park in the gravel trap. As always in a situation like this, the race had to be stopped so that the marshals could remove the unfortunate driver and his stricken car to safety, not something that is best done with 20 or more keen young Formula Fordsters arriving at racing speed like a bomb blast.

SANDHER BLASTER!

> 003> SANDHER

> 004> SANDHER

> 005> SANDHER

> 006> SANDHER

OH LOHRDY!

Formula Ford, Brands Hatch, October 1988: More Formula Ford Festival frolics as Ellen Lohr takes a novel approach to Paddock Hill Bend. This famously tricky corner at the end of the start/finish straight has caught out the very best in its time and, with so much at stake in the once-a-year Festival, would claim scalp after scalp, but few with as much elegance as this accident. Fortunately for Lohr, the car stayed level in the air, flying like a frisbee, landed four-square and didn't roll. However, perhaps as a result of this, although she walked away uninjured, the German woman turned to touring cars after this unchoreographed example of aerial ballet.

TOURING CARS

British Touring Cars, Knockhill, July 1994: Sitting high on a Scottish hillside, the Knockhill circuit could be described as being on top of the world, and this is how Alfa Romeo works driver Gabriele Tarquini felt when he arrived there, sitting at the top of the points table. He didn't qualify well, but was soon making up ground in the first race when he hit a little trouble that resulted in the most spectacular accident of the season. Luckily for the Italian, who failed to start the second race, he went on to become champion.

His spectacular sequence of barrel rolls was triggered by an impact from behind when Renault works driver Tim Harvey thought he saw a gap as Gabriele looked for a way past Rickard Rydell's Volvo estate. You know how frustrating it can be when you're stuck behind one of those... So Harvey pounced as they dived into the 90mph McIntyres right-hander, but he clipped the Alfa's right rear and Gabriele got to see the Scottish circuit as he'd never seen it before. Gabriele was extracted somewhat dazed and suffering from whiplash and bruising. Although Tim finished the race in fourth place, he was disqualified.

TURNING TARQUINI

> 001> TARQUINI   > 002> TARQUINI   > 003> TARQUINI

> 004> TARQUINI   > 005> TARQUINI

"When I saw that Tarquini wasn't getting anywhere, I had a stab down the inside. He came across to block me and I caught him"

Tim Harvey

WATCHING THE SPA-RKS FLY

Spa 24 Hours, Spa-Francorchamps, July 1992: Many consider the mighty Spa-Francorchamps circuit quite dangerous enough in its own right, its twists and turns and fast-changing weather conditions a real driving challenge. Stretch the race to 24 hours to add endurance to the mixture, then spice this up with refuelling stops to keep the mechanics on their toes and you have all the ingredients for incident.

However, few would have predicted what happened about five hours into the race when Anders Olofsson was given the 'go' signal and pulled off in his pace-setting Nissan GT-R. But it all went wrong as the car snagged the refuelling hose and this pulled over the refuelling rig, spilling fuel down the sloping pitlane. In a matter of seconds, it ignited, lighting the evening sky with 70ft flames that licked up to the balcony above the pits. Fortunately, this being Belgium, most fans had drifted off for a portion of frites et mayonnaise. Three Nissan mechanics suffered from inhaling extinguishant and minor burns but it had been a right scare and a warning to all other competitors. To make matters worse, the team's other car had retired just 15 minutes into the 24-hour race.

STELLA A

SECA

The car snagged the refuelling hose and pulled over the refuelling rig, spilling fuel

> 001> SPENCE

> 002> SPENCE

SPENCE TRIES SITTING ON THE FENCE

British Touring Cars, Oulton Park, May 1999: Racing circuits can look perfectly safe until an accident that's out of the ordinary, exposing a flaw in their armour. One such accident happened when Spence began a train of events that ended up with him taking his Renault Laguna to meet the fans. Keen as they were to meet him, they'd have preferred it if he'd not brought his car with him... The incident occurred in qualifying, on a wet track. Locking his brakes on the 120mph on the approach to Lodge corner, he spotted Alain Menu's Ford Mondeo already beached in the gravel trap. This forced him to steer to the right, thus the unusual angle of hitting the tyres and his subsequent breach of security as his car bounced off the tyre wall and straddled the safety fencing. Spence was horrified with where he'd ended up: "I got on the radio and said 'I've had a horrendous accident, I'm in the crowd'. I thought I'd killed a marshal." Thank goodness it wasn't race day when thousands of fans would have been lining the track to get close to the action.

> 003> SPENCE

> 004> SPENCE

> 001> LOWNDES

> 002> LOWNDES

> 003> LOWNDE

> 007> LOWNDES

> 008> LOWNDES

> 009> LOWNDE

> 013> LOWNDES

> 014> LOWNDES

Australian Supercar V8s, Calder Park, July 1999: Proving that even the masters of their craft can get it wrong, multiple champion Craig Lowndes went for one of the most violent rodeo rides ever seen in Australia. Having won the first of the three races, Lowndes was clipped on the run to the first corner of the second race. Doing 120mph at the time, his Holden was turned onto its roof and ran like that for 100 metres before pitching into a sequence of five flips. When the dust had settled, rival Larry Perkins was one of many who pulled up at the scene to see if they could help, but Greg Murphy was already there, helping to extract the shocked driver who'd injured one of his knees. "Once it was on the roof," said Lowndes, "all I could do was brace myself. I took my hands off the steering wheel and covered my head. Then I waited for the bang. I knew it was going to be a big one."

> 004> LOWNDES

> 005> LOWNDES

> 006> LOWNDES

> 010> LOWNDES

> 011> LOWNDES

> 012> LOWNDES

ROLL ME OVER AND DO IT AGAIN

> 015> LOWNDES

> 016> LOWNDES

Richards' Holden looked as though it was shaping up to clear the fences

> 001> RICHARDS

> 005> RICHARDS

> 006> RICHARDS

PLAYING TO THE STANDS

Australian Supercar V8s, Pukekohe, November 2003: Jason Richards may spend his year racing in Australia but his family hails from New Zealand a generation back, so no wonder he was trying particularly hard to impress when the Supercar V8 series crossed the Tasman Sea to race at Pukekohe near Auckland. With it being a horseracing venue as well, Richards behaved even more unpredictably on the grass than our four-legged friends. Then his Holden looked as though it was shaping up to clear the fences around the infield before electing to lie down for a rest on its back, like a horse with its legs in the air.

> 002> RICHARDS

> 003> RICHARDS

> 004> RICHARDS

> 007> RICHARDS

> 008> RICHARDS

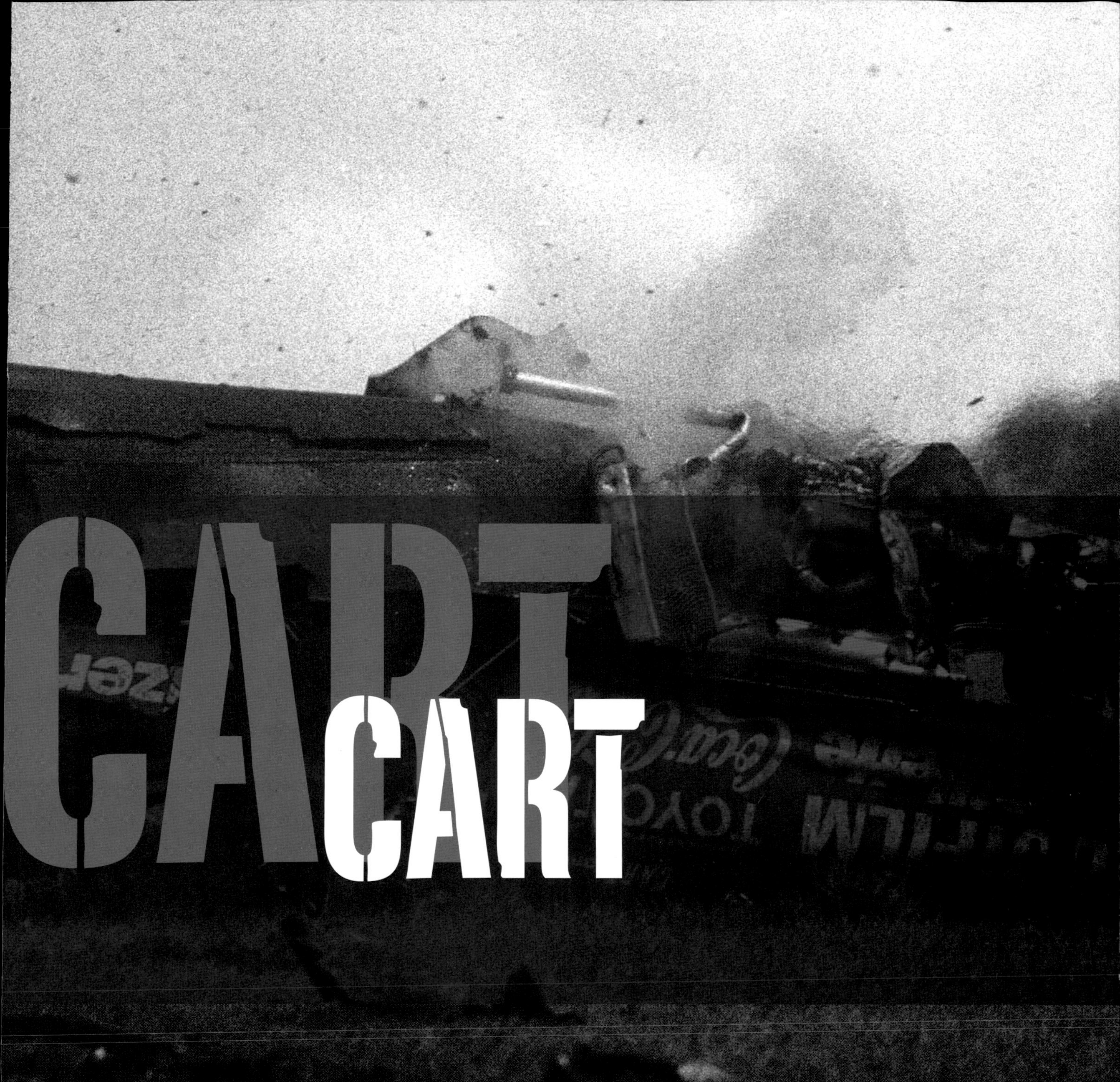

CART

MANSELL MAKES AN IMPRESSION

CART, Phoenix Int'l Raceway, April 1993: Nigel Mansell wanted to burst onto the CART scene in a big way fresh from winning the Formula 1 world title in 1992. But even this ultimate showman hadn't meant to be this flashy, crashing at 170mph at Turn 1 and punching a hole in the outside wall... "It was the worst crash of my career," he exclaimed from hospital. "The back end went away. I was on the throttle at the time. It was a big impact. I said to myself, 'there's no way I can get it back'. So I ducked down. The next thing that I remember is waking up in the helicopter just as it was landing." He bounced back to win the title...

"The back end got away. I said to myself, 'there's no way I can get it back'. So I ducked down"

Nigel Mansell

>   **001> ATLANTA**

>   **004> ATLANTA**   >   **005> ATLANTA**

ATLANTA'S
DIRTY DOZEN

Indy Racing League, Atlanta Motor Speedway, April 2001: Every now and then, a driver on an oval has an accident then decides it's not fair that the others are missing out on the fun. This was one of those, but unusually it was not caused by a driver losing control. On this occasion, it was by a driver slowing down... Cory Witherill was the culprit, marking his first race in the IRL by doing so unexpectedly in front of Felipe Giaffone at Turn 4. Then the fun started as he sent Casey Mears into a spin and car after car was caught out as they jinked and dived in attempted avoidance. Robbie Buhl (24) thumped the wall, with Jack Miller's car (11) providing the pyrotechnics. They were joined in the melee by Billy Boat, Jon Herb, Sarah Fisher, Al Unser Jr., Davey Hamilton, Jeret Schroeder and Robby McGehee. Amazingly, only Miller was injured, being concussed. Scarily, a liberated wheel made its way into the grandstand. Fortunately, it was in a closed-off sector, but it stressed the danger of airborne debris, emphasising why safety fences need to be so high at circuits on which cars hit 240mph.

Every now and then, a driver has an accident then decides it's not fair that others are missing out on the fun

WHEN PUSH COMES TO SHOVE OFF

CART, Indianapolis 500, May 1989: Winning the Indy 500 ranks right at the top of any driver's hit list, even for drivers as illustrious as two-time Formula 1 champion Emerson Fittipaldi or Al Unser Jr. Neither at this point had won America's biggest race, though, and this was the result of their dogfight. Imagine the scene: they're way out front and it's lap 199 of 200, Unser Jr. is ahead, Fittipaldi hoping to find a way past. Then they hit traffic down the back straight. Fittipaldi explains how it was that his rival ended up in the wall at Turn 3 and he went on to collect that famous trophy: "I was on the inside line and I wasn't going to back off. We touched wheels and he went off into the wall. I almost spun, too. It was a big moment." Angry at the time, Unser Jr later acknowledged it as a racing accident: "I wasn't going to lift and Emerson didn't lift either..." The result was inevitable.

A ROCKY MOUNTAIN HIGH

CART, Denver, September 2002: Hitting another car is never a good way to impress. Hitting your own team-mate and taking them out of the race ranks even lower on the scale of polite things to do. Yet this is what Paul Tracy saw fit to do when the CART circus visited the Rockies. He and fellow Team Green racer Dario Franchitti had been at sea in qualifying and knew that they had a lot of ground to make up in the race. Trouble was, Tracy tried to do it all on the opening lap with a banzai outbraking manoeuvre that led to him clouting Franchitti's car hard enough to force it into retirement and narrowly missing Oriol Servia's car as he flew through the air. Franchitti was not impressed. "I talked to Paul and some of the other guys around us on the grid before the start," said the Scot, "and I told Paul 'if you've got a quick car, be on your merry way'. Then he wiped me out on the first lap…"

"I told Paul 'if you've got a quick car, be on your merry way'. Then he wiped me out…"

EXPLOSIVE ACTION!

CART, Elkhart Lake, August 2001: Smashes on ovals can last a long time as the wrecks and their debris skid along the wall and down the banking, but Memo Gidley demonstrates here at the tricky Road America circuit that those on road courses can be every bit as violent. Gidley got out of shape when jockeying for position shortly after a restart and did something that no one would wish to do: he smacked his car into a bridge parapet at 145mph. The explosion on impact was truly massive, as his car rolled over onto its rool hoop, scattering debris in its wake.

Gidley did something that no-one would wish to do:
he smacked his car into a bridge parapet at 145mph

001> GIDLEY

004> GIDLEY

002> GIDLEY

003> GIDLEY

005> GIDLEY

006> GIDLEY

This was no oval-style hit and slide along the wall routine, though, but a full, head-on impact that all but ripped the front off the Chip Ganassi Racing Reynard. Scott Dixon, following closely behind, was presented with a cloud of debris and was hit on the helmet by Gidley's rear wing (shown at the bottom of photos 5 and 6) which then took off his rear wing. Although he had to be cut from the wreckage, the accident easily could have been so much worse. Luckily for Gidley, as he gathered his thoughts in hospital and nursed a fractured right arm and bruised knees as he contemplated his racing return, he had absolutely 'no memory' of this violent accident.

CART, Nazareth, May 2000: Picking up a puncture when racing on an oval is nobody's idea of fun, as it leads to a sudden inability to turn and an all but inevitable collision with the wall. Ouch! So, when debris is spread following an accident no one minds if the safety car comes out while the track is brushed clean to be sure that no driver hits a jagged shard with the aforementioned consequences. Unfortunately, a lengthy period spent lapping at reduced speed behind a safety car leads to a reduction in heat in the cars' tyres. This means a loss of grip and makes full bore cornering something of a risk when the all-clear is given and the pack is released to race again.

This brain-rattling, wheel-shedding crash sequence involving Mark Blundell and Helio Castroneves happened when the field had just been released after a period behind the safety car, with Brazilian hitting the rear of the Englishman's Motorola-liveried Reynard, sending both into the wall. Note how Paul Tracy is able to keep low and stay out of trouble. Blundell was livid: "I can't believe that he tried to make a move on me there." As ever in racing, the other driver saw it differently, with Castroneves saying: "I got halfway in front of him. He was already a lap down and I thought he'd give me room, but he came down on me and we hit, then went up into the wall."

NAZARETH'S MIRACLE ESCAPE

"I got halfway in front of him. He was a lap down and I thought he'd give me room, but he came down on me"

Helio Castroneves

YOU SPIN ME ROUND

CART, Rockingham, September 2001: Water seeping through the track surface of this all-new circuit looked set to scupper the first CART championship round in Britain, with delay following delay as the race organisers attempted to sort out the problem. However, finally, it was "gentlemen, start your engines" and all stations go and Max Papis gave the fans in the grandstands a first taste of high-speed spinning by losing it out of Turn 4 and gyrating in a wreath of tyre smoke all the way down the start/finish straight. He did a great job in keeping it away from the walls, but Burno Junqueira and Tora Takagi fell off in avoidance.

> 002> JOURDAIN

CART, Rockingham, September 2001: No oval is like another. They may look similar, but each has its quirks and the CART Championship Series' first visit to the Rockingham speedway in England gave drivers a chance to master something new, or not... The result was a host of drivers going for a spin, particularly out of Turn 4, a corner that required a little lift. British driver Dario Franchitti didn't spin there, but he certainly got to look into the eyes of someone who did: Michel Jourdain. "We soon got into lapping traffic," said the Scot, "and Michel spun right in front of me in Turn 4. That's the closest I've ever been to something like that without being involved! I was on the brakes, saw a gap, off the brakes, gap vanished, on the brakes and he's coming up the track towards me. I got on the power and just made it by." Team-mate Michael Andretti also got closer to the spinning Mexican than he would have liked.

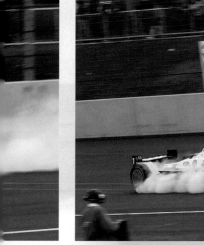

002> PAPIS

> 003> PAPIS

> 004> PAPIS

"I was on the brakes, saw a gap, off the brakes, gap vanished, on the brakes and he's coming up towards me"

Dario Franchitti

SPORTS CARS

> 002> MASS

> 003> MASS

> 004> MASS

JOCHEN
GETS IT MASS-IVELY WRONG

He found his front wheels coming off the ground as he approached Woodcote at 175mph...

>   001> MASS

World Championship of Makes, Silverstone, May 1979: Here's a moment that the photographer in the firing line is unlikely to forget. The car bouncing towards him was a two-time winner of the Le Mans 24 Hours. It was in the lead by miles. But that didn't stop it from destroying itself against the barriers at his feet. The car in question was the works Porsche 936 with Jochen Mass at the wheel. Co-driver Brian Redman had already suffered the loss of rear brakes at 185mph, as he approached Stowe corner but escaped with just rear bodywork damage from clipping a couple of catchfencing poles. "I've had three major accidents in my career," he reported, "and they've all been down to a mechanical failure." After a lengthy stop in the pits for new brakes pads and new rear bodywork, which had to be wired on, Mass resumed. Late in the race, he too had a massive fright when he found his front wheels coming off the ground as he approached Woodcote at 175mph... He spun rapidly several times then slammed into the barriers. It's thought that either the rear bodywork worked itself loose or a rear tyre deflated, but the outcome was rather more than a little dramatic. Had the massively experienced German driver not had so much car around him, he could well not have lived to tell the tale.

>   005> MASS

FLYING THE WEBBER WAY

Le Mans 24 Hours, June 1999: Automotive manufacturers love to win this classic French enduro as it gives them bragging rights that their cars are not only the fastest but the toughest. Porsche has basked in its wins there for decades with Jaguar and Mercedes also making the most of their successes. But the German manufacturer experienced the flip side of the coin in 1999 when their cars had an inability to stay connected with terra firma. Mark Webber had survived a dramatic flap on the flat-out, 220mph Mulsanne Straight in qualifying, then suffered a near identical somersault in the warm-up on race morning. To make matters worse, Mercedes' motorsport bosses elected to modify the cars and race on, only for Peter Dumbreck to fly into the trees in one of the sister cars.

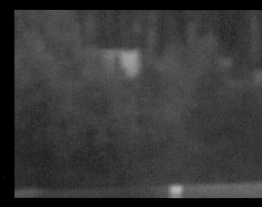

> 001> WEBBER

> 002> WEBBER

> 005> WEBBER

> 006> WEBBER

"I just turned to open the window flap and when I looked back I couldn't see the track, only the sky"

Mark Webber

Webber claimed that his first aerial detour had been "a bad cocktail of bumps and no downforce on the front" but he remains unclear to this day as to what happened to trigger the second, the one shown here. Despite there being no car immediately ahead of him to steal the air from the nose of his CLR, and thus the downforce, the Australian's car clearly got light over the crest, the nose lifted and it started a backwards flip that came back to ground oh so close to landing on a Dodge Viper. Thankful for the structural integrity of the CLR, Webber lived to fight another day, suffering just light bruising.

...AND FINALLY

Had Corner been wearing belts, he mightn't have lived as his Ferrari landed upside down with no roll hoop

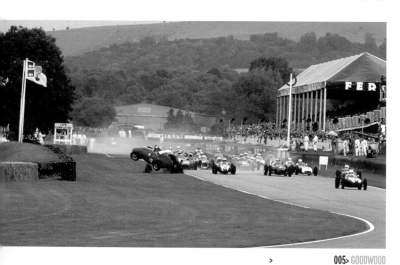

Goodwood Revival meeting, Goodwood, September 2000: Historic motorsport is a massive growth area, with fans all around the globe flocking to see the cars of yesteryear in action, as a trip down memory lane for the older fans and as an education for the next generation. Yet, whatever the glamour of these cars, they are raced now as they were then, offering the drivers a vastly inferior level of safety, with many not fitted with roll hoops and, in keeping with the age, no seat belts. It's a hard call to make, as it would be almost sacreligious to modernise the cars and remove their soul. So it's up to the drivers to compete with a little in reserve to offer a margin of safety.

> 003> GOODWOOD

> 004> GOODWOOD

> 007> GOODWOOD

> 008> GOODWOOD

> 011> GOODWOOD

> 012> GOODWOOD

This sequence showing Nigel Corner being thrown 10 metres into the air is the most shocking in this entire book, as the only one in which a driver is thrown out of the car, showing how safety standards have advanced. Better still, driver Corner fits in with the title "And They Walked Away..." as he did, albeit only after a spell in hospital. In fact, had he been wearing safety belts, he might not have lived as his 1960 F1 Ferrari landed upside down, with no roll hoop, after being hit at the start. He actually landed on his feet, but then collapsed and waited for the medical crew to arrive. Amazingly, he suffered no more than broken ribs and a punctured lung. Nigel keeps these oustanding photographs on display in a bathroom at home. They make a fine laxative..

ACKNOWLEDGEMENTS

The following photographers or agencies captured the dramatic moments captured in this book: The Autocar Collection, 122-123; Lorenzo Bellanca, 16-17; Jeff Bloxham, 2-3, 6, 28-29, 48-51, 90-91, 92-93, 96-97, 124-127, 132-135, 138-139, 144-147; Michael C Brown, 108; Charles Coates, 19, 26-27, 40-43; DPPI, 8-9, 136-137, 140-143; Glen Dunbar, 130-131; John Dunbar, 38, 58-59; Martyn Elford, 60, 94-95; Steve Etherington, 18; Getty Images, 10-11, 34-37, 98-101, 104-105, 120-124; Malcolm Griffiths, 44-45; Darren Heath, 20-21; Leland Hill, 109; Keith Howes, 39; Jeff Hutchinson, 56-57; Loran Hygema, 102-103, 110-113; Robert LeSieur, 4-5, 62-85, 87; Michael Levitt, 114-117; Picme, 22-25; Pascal Rondeau/Getty, 48-49; Clive Rose, 120-121; Peter Spinney, 118-119; Michael Tee, 38, 61; Steven Tee, 12-15, 30-31, 47, 52-55; John Townsend, 32-33; Bryn Williams, 128-129; Peirce Williams, 86, 88-89, 106-107.

INDEX

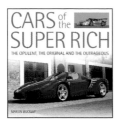

Cars of the Super Rich
ISBN: 0-7603-1953-7

Star, Cars & Infamy:
100 Stories of the Bad, the Daft,
and the Deadly
ISBN: 0-7603-1687-2

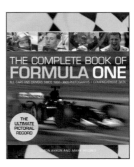

The Complete Book of
Formula One
ISBN: 0-7603-1688-0

The Complete Book of the
World Rally Champions
ISBN: 0-7603-1954-5

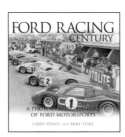

Ford Racing Century:
A Photographic History of
Ford Motorsports
ISBN: 0-7603-1621-X

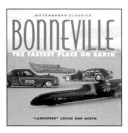

Bonneville:
The Fastest Place on Earth
ISBN: 0-7603-1372-5

Jack Brabham Story
ISBN: 0-7603-1590-6

Kurtis Kraft:
Masterworks of Speed and Style
ISBN: 0-7603-0910-8

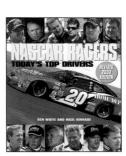

NASCAR Racers:
Today's Top Drivers
ISBN: 0-7603-1392-X